# The Edible, Green Machine

Happy House

# About Wise & Wide

- A systematic 6-level English reading program based on Lexile® measures
- Diverse and interesting topics chosen from the elementary curriculums of Korea and English speaking western countries
- Well-written books in various forms including fiction stories, descriptive texts, and classics retold
- The informative but original fiction stories grab your interest, leading to the easy and clear understanding of the educational content.
- Improve thinking skills with solid after-reading activities at all levels of the series.

**Wise & Wide** is a 6-level English reading program that consists of 60 books and each level is systematically divided by Lexile® measures. The Lexile® Framework for Reading is the most popular reading measuring system in American formal education curriculums and many English programs. Over 20 out of 50 states in the U.S. mark Lexile® measures directly on students' final report cards and over 300 well-known publishers adopt and use Lexile® measures.

Experience many kinds of readings written by professional writers from the U.S. and England. They used interesting topics that were carefully chosen after analyzing elementary curriculums from around the world including Korea, the U.S., England, and Australia among many others. Comprehensive after-reading activities including graphic organizers, speaking tasks, and After-reading Tests are ready for you.

### Levels in the series and their corresponding Lexile® measures

| Level | Lexile® measures | U.S. Grade |
|---|---|---|
| Level 1 | Below 200L | Pre K - K |
| Level 2 | 190L - 400L | Lower Grade 1 |
| Level 3 | 350L - 530L | Upper Grade 1 |
| Level 4 | 420L - 650L | Grade 2 |
| Level 5 | 520L - 940L | Grade 3 - 4 |
| Level 6 | 830L - 1070L | Grade 5 - 6 |

\* Smart Readers: Wise & Wide level 1 is applicable to the preschool level in the U.S.

\* The source of the relationship between Lexile® measures and U.S. school grades: CCSS(Common Core State Standards) FOR ENGLISH LANGUAGE ARTS, APPENDIX A (2012, which is used by 45 states in the U.S.)

# Topic List

| | Level 1 | Level 2 | Level 3 | Level 4 | Level 5 | Level 6 |
|---|---|---|---|---|---|---|
| **Book 1** | Science>Biology: The hibernation of animals<br>Story | Science>Biology: Living and nonliving things<br>Story | Science>Biology> Animals & the Environment: Sea otters<br>Story | Environment> Living with nature: The diver & the persimmon tree<br>Story | Science>Biology> Animal: Amazing animals of the Amazon<br>Story | Science>Biology: Germs, transmitted diseases<br>Story |
| **Book 2** | Literature> World classics: Aesop's fables<br>Story | Literature> Traditional fairy tale: Old tales about stones<br>Story | Social Studies> Economy: To run a business to make and save money<br>Story | Science>Biology> Plants: Photosynthesis<br>Story | Science>Earth science: Earth's layers,earthquakes, volcanoes, and earth's atmosphere<br>Report | Mathematics> Sequence: The golden ratio & the Fibonacci sequence<br>Story |
| **Book 3** | Science>Physics: How shadows are formed<br>Story | Literature> World classics: Peter Pan<br>Story | Science>Scientific technology: Nanobots<br>Story | Literature>Myths: World's creation stories<br>Story | Literature> Legend: The story of King Arthur<br>Story | |
| **Book 4** | Literature> Traditional literature: The Talmud<br>Story | Science>Biology> Animal: Polar bears<br>Story | Science>Biology> Animal: Mountain gorillas<br>Story | Social Studies> Cultural anthropology: Amazing ancient cultures of the world<br>Story | Science> Earth science: Clouds and weather<br>Story | |
| **Book 5** | | | Social Studies> Cultural anthropology: Astonishing festivals<br>Report | Art>Music: Stories from two operas<br>Story | | |
| **Book 6** | | | | Social Studies> People: Three great people who overcame hardships<br>Story | | |
| **Book 7** | | | | | | |
| **Book 8** | | | | | | |
| **Book 9** | | | | | | |
| **Book 10** | | | | | | |

* 10 books in each level will be published.

# How to Use This Book

**•Before Reading**

You can easily find the topic and what kind of story you are about to read.

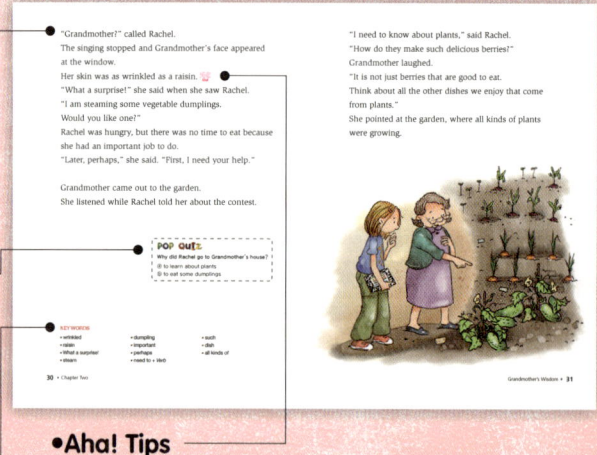

**•The text**

All the stories were written by professional writers from the U.S. and England, so you will read authentic and appropriate English sentences and expressions in every book in the series.

**•Pop Quiz**

Check out right away if you understand what you have just read by solving a pop quiz that checks your comprehension.

**•Key Words**

The key words and expressions on each page are listed for you to easily study them.

**•Aha! Tips**

Download free Korean explanations at *www.ihappyhouse.co.kr* for all of the sentences marked with "Aha!". These explain cultural, scientific, and economic knowledge or they deal with aspects of English such as grammatical structures or idiomatic expressions. There are lots of "Aha! Tips" to help you understand the text.

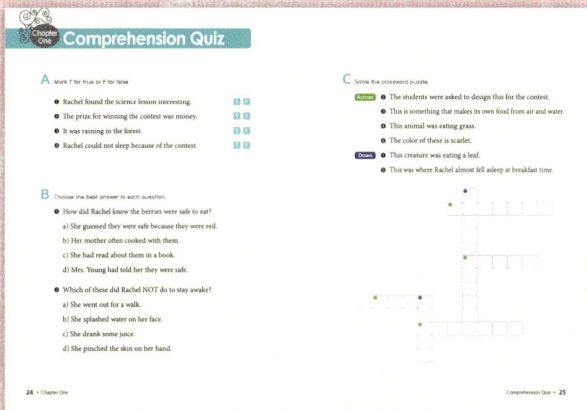

## •Comprehension Quiz

After reading one chapter, solve various questions to find out if you fully understand the content.

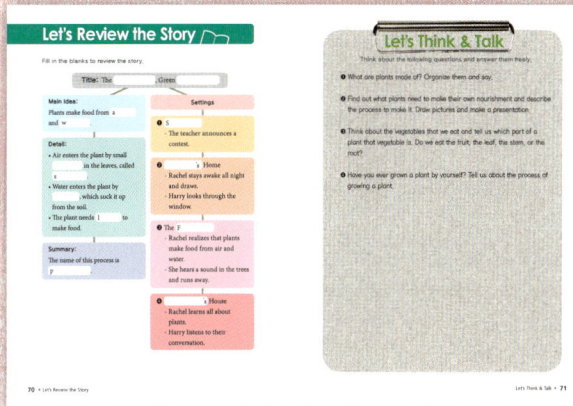

## •Let's Review the Story /
## •Let's Think & Talk

Fill in the blanks in the organizer to summarize the whole story. Express your own thinking and feelings about the story by answering the questions. You can build up logic and reasoning skills for your essay examinations in the future.

## Appendix

### Audio CD

In the CD audio book form, the texts are read vividly by American professional voice actors.

### After-reading Test

Solve an additionally provided After-reading Test for each book.

### The Korean translation, Answer Keys, a Word Quiz, a Word List, and Aha! Tips for each book

You can download them for free at *www.ihappyhouse.co.kr*

# Before Reading

## The Edible, Green Machine

Level 4-2,
Lexile® 520L

•Science)Biology)Plants
•Story

## What do plants eat?

We often can see animals eat food. But how about plants? Plants are also living things so they must take nourishment. Then how and what nourishment do they take?

Plants also take nourishment from nature! But they take something different from what animals and humans do. What plants take from nature is sunlight, water and $CO_2$, one of the gases in the air. A plant's leaves have cells that digest sunlight well, which the plant uses for energy to produce a sugar-like material for its nourishment. The cells gather sunlight and then mix water that comes through the plant's root with $CO_2$ that comes through air holes on the leaves to produce the material like sugar for its nourishment. The process is called "photosynthesis." In the book, let's find out in more detail how such a process happens in a plant.

## Summary

Rachel is a smart girl who likes going to botanical gardens and amusement parks the most!

One day, Rachel knew that the prize for the school contest was a free pass for a botanical garden and an amusement park, so she decided to win the contest. To win it, she had to invent or find a special machine that can make food with air and water. Rachel didn't have any clue what on earth it meant and became worried. Fortunately, she came up with an idea while walking in a forest and was pleased. But someone was peeking at what she was doing! Who was it? Will Rachel be able to win the contest?

# Contents

## The Edible, Green Machine

# The Edible,
# Green Machine

# A Fright in the Forest

# Chapter One

Rachel sat at the back of her class and yawned.

The science lesson was dull this morning.

The teacher's voice made her feel sleepy.

But then the teacher said something that made Rachel
sit up and listen.

"We are going to have a contest," Mrs. Young said.

"There will be a prize for the winner."

"What is the prize?" asked Harry.

He always wanted to win every contest there was. Aha!

Mrs. Young smiled.

"The prize will be a free ticket to visit the botanic
gardens and amusement park," she said.

**KEY WORDS**

- fright
- at the back
- yawn
- dull (= boring)

- sit up (sit-sat-sat)
- have a contest (have-had-had)
- winner
- free

- visit
- botanic garden
- amusement park

When she heard this, Rachel was very excited.
She loved the botanic gardens, which had plants from
all around the world, and she loved the amusement park
even more!
"What do we have to do to win the contest?" she said.
Mrs. Young looked around the class.
"I want you all to invent or find a special machine.
Then you must explain how it works."
"What kind of machine?" asked Harry.
"A machine that can make food from air and water,"
said Mrs. Young.

▲ Kew Gardens
(the largest botanic garden)

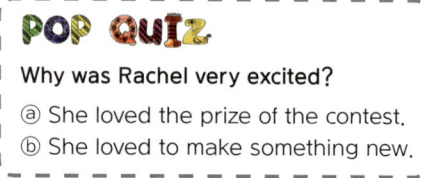

**Why was Rachel very excited?**
ⓐ She loved the prize of the contest.
ⓑ She loved to make something new.

### KEY WORDS

- excited
- all around the world
- even more
- look around

- invent
- machine
- must
- explain

- work
- kind
- make from
  (make-made-made)

"Surely that's impossible!" gasped Rachel.

But Harry smiled to himself.

He took out a piece of paper and a pencil and began to draw a diagram.

**KEY WORDS**

- surely
- impossible (↔ possible)
- gasp
- smile to oneself

- take out (take-took-taken)
- a piece of paper
- draw (draw-drew-drawn)
- diagram

Rachel thought about the contest all the way home.

She thought all through the family mealtime.

She was still thinking when she went to bed.

"You are very quiet," said her mother.

"Are you ill?"

"No," said Rachel, "I am just thinking."

Rachel could not sleep.

The house was quiet and dark.

Only the faint glow of the moon shone through her window.

She got out of bed and tore a sheet of paper from her notebook.

Rachel began to draw.

She shook her head, sighed, and crumpled up the piece of paper.

She took another sheet and started again.

**KEY WORDS**

- all the way
- all through
- mealtime
- ill
- faint
- glow
- shine (shine-shone-shone)
- through
- get out of bed (get-got-gotten)
- tear (tear-tore-torn)
- sheet
- shake one's head (shake-shook-shaken)
- sigh
- crumple up
- another

**POP QUIZ**

Why could Rachel not sleep?

ⓐ She was ill.

ⓑ She was thinking about the contest.

When the sun came up, there were balls of paper all over the floor.

Rachel was very tired and wanted to go to sleep.

She was glad that it was the weekend, so she did not have to go to school.

A tap at the window made her jump. 📖 Aha!

"Who is it?" she called.

Harry's face appeared.

"Have you come up with a plan yet?" he said.

Rachel shook her head.

"Not yet. Have you?"

"I'm working on it," said Harry.

He walked away, whistling as he went.

**KEY WORDS**

- **come up** (come-came-come)
- ball
- all over the floor
- tired
- tap
- jump
- call

- appear
- come up with
- yet
- work on
- walk away
- whistle
- as

At breakfast time, Rachel almost fell asleep at the table.

When she went to splash cool water on her face, she almost fell asleep at the sink.

She pinched the skin on the back of her hand.

"Wake up!" she told herself.

"You have some hard thinking to do today."

In order to stay alert, she decided to go out for a walk.

She took her notebook and pencils with her.

All the time, she tried to think of a machine that could make food out of air and water.

*What would it be made of?*

*How would it work?*

---

**KEY WORDS**

- fall asleep (fall-fell-fallen)
- splash
- sink
- pinch
- hard thinking
- in order to

- stay
- alert
- decide
- go out for a walk (go-went-gone)
- all the time
- make (out) of

The fresh, sweet air made Rachel feel wide awake.

She saw some birds pecking at seeds on the ground.

She saw a goat chewing on fresh green grass.

She even found a tiny striped caterpillar eating a juicy green leaf. Aha!

▲ caterpillar

KEY WORDS

- feel wide awake (feel-felt-felt)
- peck
- seed
- goat
- chew on
- striped
- caterpillar
- juicy

Further along the path, there was a bush full of scarlet berries.

Rachel knew that these berries were safe to eat because her mother often cooked with them.

She picked a handful and put them into her mouth, and she enjoyed the sweet flavor on her tongue.

"Wait a minute!" gasped Rachel.

She looked at the birds, the goat, and the caterpillar.

"You are all eating food," she said as she pointed at each one in turn, "but where did that food come from? It was not made in a factory or in a shop. 📖 Aha! It was not cooked in a kitchen or in a restaurant."

She looked down at the berries in her hand and smiled.

"Nobody made these berries, but they are delicious to eat. And where do they come from?"

The birds went on pecking at the seeds, and the goat went on chewing the grass.

The caterpillar went on eating the leaf.

In a few minutes, the leaf was all gone.

**KEY WORDS**

| | | |
|---|---|---|
| • further | • handful | • factory |
| • along | • flavor | • nobody |
| • path | • point at | • delicious |
| • bush | • each one | • go on |
| • full of | • in turn | • in a few minutes |
| • scarlet berries | • come from | • gone |

"Plants!" shouted Rachel.

She threw the berries in the air, and they showered down around her.

"Plants make food out of fresh air and water."

She danced about, skipped, and laughed.

"I can win the contest!

The answer was in front of me the whole time!"

But then she stopped as she remembered Mrs. Young's voice and the second part of the contest.

Now she had to explain how the plant made food, but she didn't know.

A sudden crack made Rachel jump.

It came from the forest along the edge of the path.

"Who is there?" she called.

Nobody answered.

Rachel gave a nervous laugh.

Her heart thumped like a fist punching her ribs.

"It is only a deer stepping on a twig," she told herself.

Then, she heard a whispering sound as if something
was moving through the forest toward her.

Rachel did not wait to see what it was.

She ran away down the path
with her arms moving
like windmills.

**A** Mark T for true or F for false.

❶ Rachel found the science lesson interesting. T F

❷ The prize for winning the contest was money. T F

❸ It was raining in the forest. T F

❹ Rachel could not sleep because of the contest. T F

**B** Choose the best answer to each question.

❶ How did Rachel know the berries were safe to eat?

a) She guessed they were safe because they were red.

b) Her mother often cooked with them.

c) She had read about them in a book.

d) Mrs. Young had told her they were safe.

❷ Which of these did Rachel NOT do to stay awake?

a) She went out for a walk.

b) She splashed water on her face.

c) She drank some juice.

d) She pinched the skin on her hand.

**C** Solve the crossword puzzle.

**Across**  ❷ The students were asked to design this for the contest.

❸ This is something that makes its own food from air and water.

❹ This animal was eating grass.

❻ The color of these is scarlet.

**Down**  ❶ This creature was eating a leaf.

❺ This was where Rachel almost fell asleep at breakfast time.

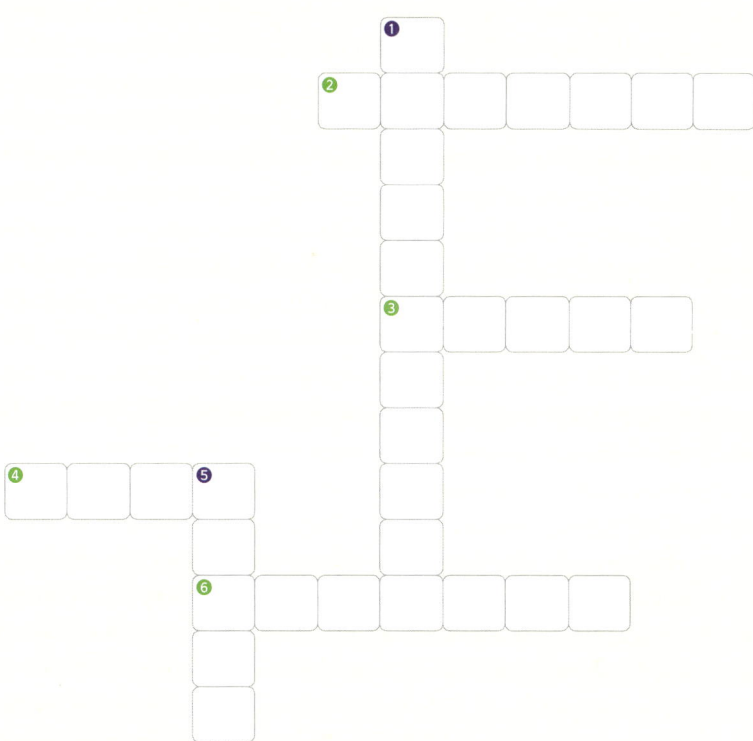

# Chapter Two

# Grandmother's Wisdom

After a while, Rachel stopped running.

She gasped for breath, and her legs felt weak.

She turned round and saw Harry running up behind her.

He was laughing so hard that his face was red.

"It was you!" shouted Rachel.

"Why did you hide in the forest to frighten me?"

Harry stopped laughing, but he would not look at Rachel.

"I was just out for a walk," he said as he stared at the ground.

"You were spying on me," said Rachel as she jabbed a finger at his chest.

**KEY WORDS**

- wisdom
- after a while
- gasp for breath
- turn round
- run up behind
- hide (hide-hid-hidden)
- frighten
- stare at
- spy on
- jab

"You want to find out what I'm going to do for the contest. You want to cheat."

Harry knocked her hand out of the way.

"Don't talk nonsense," he said, and away he ran, back down the path.

Rachel decided to go to Grandmother's house.

"She has a vegetable garden," said Rachel.

"She will help me to learn about plants."

Grandmother was a modern woman and very intelligent.

Grandmother's house was also very modern.

It looked as though it belonged in a city, not a forest.

The windows were wide open, and Rachel could hear a voice singing.

**KEY WORDS**

- vegetable garden
- modern
- intelligent
- as though
- belong

Who makes the plants grow where nobody sees?

Who sends water to the tallest trees?

Who calls the seed to send out roots?

And who gives color to the tender shoots?

**KEY WORDS**

- **grow** (grow-grew-grown)
- **tallest**
- **send out roots** (send-sent-sent)
- **tender shoot**

"Grandmother?" called Rachel.

The singing stopped and Grandmother's face appeared at the window.

Her skin was as wrinkled as a raisin.

"What a surprise!" she said when she saw Rachel.

"I am steaming some vegetable dumplings.

Would you like one?"

Rachel was hungry, but there was no time to eat because she had an important job to do.

"Later, perhaps," she said. "First, I need your help."

Grandmother came out to the garden.

She listened while Rachel told her about the contest.

---

## POP QUIZ

**Why did Rachel go to Grandmother's house?**

ⓐ to learn about plants

ⓑ to eat some dumplings

---

**KEY WORDS**

- wrinkled
- raisin
- What a surprise!
- steam
- dumpling
- important
- perhaps
- need to + *Verb*
- such
- dish
- all kinds of

"I need to know about plants," said Rachel.

"How do they make such delicious berries?"

Grandmother laughed.

"It is not just berries that are good to eat.

Think about all the other dishes we enjoy that come from plants."

She pointed at the garden, where all kinds of plants were growing.

Rachel broke off a spinach leaf and put it in her mouth.

"We can eat leaves as well as berries," she said.

Grandmother dug deep in the soil and found some thick orange roots.

She gave one to Rachel.

"Carrots!" gasped Rachel.

"I did not know they were roots."

"We eat the leaves of some plants," said Grandmother.

"We eat the roots, berries, or seeds of other plants. Sometimes even the flowers are edible, which means we can eat them."

She pointed at a plant which had wide leaves that were like hands.

Each plant had large orange flowers, some of them with a zucchini in the center.

▲ zucchini

"Can we eat the zucchini flowers?" asked Rachel.

"Of course. They taste delicious when I stir-fry them," said Grandmother, licking her lips.

"What about zucchini?" said Rachel.

"It is not a leaf. It is not a root, and it is not a berry. What is it?"

"It is a fruit," replied Grandmother. (Aha!)

"You may pick one if you like."

**KEY WORDS**

- **break off** (break-broke-broken)
- **spinach**
- **as well as**
- **dig** (dig-dug-dug)
- **soil**
- **thick** (↔ thin)

- **edible**
- **mean**
- **zucchini**
- **stir-fry**
- **lick one's lips**
- **reply**

Rachel took hold of the long green zucchini.

She pulled it off the plant.

"It cannot be a fruit," she said.

"Fruit is sweet, like apples or melons."

Grandmother shook her head.

"That is not always true.

A tomato is a fruit, and so is a cucumber."

Rachel sighed. There was so much to learn.

"So how do I know what is a fruit and what is not?"

"It is easy to tell.

Cut the zucchini in half and tell me what you find."

Rachel cut the zucchini in half.

It was filled with pale seeds.

"Mostly, the fruit is the part of the plant where the seeds are," explained Grandmother. (Aha!)

Suddenly, Grandmother shouted.

"Who is that?" she said as she pointed over the fence.

"Somebody is there."

Rachel guessed it was Harry.

She pressed a finger to her lips.

She crept toward the fence, but she could not see anyone there.

The forest was still.

Only the wind moved in the high branches of the trees.

Where was Harry?

Grandmother tapped Rachel on the shoulder.

She nodded toward a bush on the far side of the path.

Rachel saw the tip of a shoe poking out from beneath the bush.

Harry must be hiding there.

## POP QUIZ

**Why did Rachel press her finger to her lips?**

ⓐ She wanted Grandmother to be quiet.
ⓑ She had a sore mouth.

**KEY WORDS**

- fence
- press a finger to one's lips
- creep (creep-crept-crept)
- anyone
- still
- nod
- the far side
- tip
- poke out
- beneath

"I am glad you are teaching me about cooking, Grandmother," said Rachel in a loud voice.

"It is so interesting that I may not enter the contest at all."

The bush trembled, and Rachel giggled to think of Harry hiding there.

"If Harry thinks I am not interested in the contest, then perhaps he might leave me alone!" she thought.

**KEY WORDS**

- interesting
- enter the contest (= join the contest)
- tremble
- giggle
- be interested in

**A** Match each sentence with the right person.

 ❶

· · a) I followed Rachel.

❷

· · b) I am intelligent. I have wrinkled skin.

❸

· · c) I am so busy that I can't eat dumplings.

**B** Fill in each blank with the right word below to complete the paragraph.

| surprised | song | Grandmother | dumpling |
|---|---|---|---|

When Rachel arrived, ❶ _____ was singing a ❷ _____.

She was ❸ _____ to see Rachel and offered her a steamed

❹ _____ to eat. But Rachel did not want one.

**C** Choose the best answer to each question.

**❶** Why did Rachel NOT want to eat the vegetable dumplings?

a) She was not hungry.

b) She did not like them.

c) She wanted to learn about plants first.

d) She knew that Grandmother was a bad cook.

**❷** How can you know whether something is a fruit or not?

a) A fruit has seeds in it.

b) A fruit always tastes sweet.

c) A fruit is always brightly colored.

d) A fruit is always round.

**❸** Why was there a shoe poking out of the bush?

a) Someone had dropped it there.

b) Grandmother kept her shoes there.

c) Harry was hiding there.

d) Rachel had taken her shoes off there.

# Nature Is Not in a Hurry

Grandmother put some plants on the kitchen table.

"The plant makes food in the leaves," she said.

"The food is a kind of sugar."

Rachel drew as many different leaves as she could.

She took out her pack of colored pencils and tried to

copy the exact shades of green.

"Why are the leaves green?" she asked.

"There is something in the leaves called *chlorophyll*," said Grandmother.

"Chloro... what?"

Rachel did not know how to spell a difficult word like that.

"Chlorophyll. It traps the sunlight, which the leaves need to make their food."

Rachel knew that plants grew much better on warm, sunny days than when it was dark and cold.

"Chlorophyll is green," said Grandmother.

She reached for a carrot.

"Don't eat that!" begged Rachel.

"I have not drawn it yet."

**KEY WORDS**

| | | |
|---|---|---|
| ▪ in a hurry | ▪ exact | ▪ better |
| ▪ a kind of | ▪ shade of | ▪ reach for |
| ▪ sugar | ▪ chlorophyll | ▪ beg |
| ▪ pack | ▪ spell | |
| ▪ copy | ▪ trap | |

Grandmother held up a carrot and an onion.

"Look how different these roots are," she said.

"The carrot has one thick and strong root. The onion has lots of thin roots, which look like wool.

They both suck up water from the soil."

Now Rachel knew that plants made food from air and water.

She also knew that plants made food in their leaves.

"But how does the water get to the leaves?" she asked.

## POP QUIZ

Why did Grandmother hold up a carrot and an onion?

ⓐ She wanted to eat them.

ⓑ She wanted to show their roots to Rachel.

**KEY WORDS**

- lots of
- wool
- suck up
- get to
- put down (↔ pick up)

- stem
- celery
- snap
- pour
- food dye

- broken
- closely
- happen
- patient

Grandmother put down the roots and picked up a stem of celery.

It made a loud crack as she snapped it in half.

She poured some red food dye into a bowl of water.

The water turned red, too.

Grandmother put the broken end of the stem into the red water.

"Watch closely, and you will see what happens," she said.

"I cannot see anything," said Rachel.

"You must be patient. Nature is not in a hurry."

Rachel drummed her fingers on the table.

She sighed, grumbled, and walked up and down the room.

"When will I see it?" she complained.

Grandmother just smiled and leaned back in her chair.

At last, Rachel could wait no longer.

She lifted the celery stem out of the bowl.

There must be something wrong with her eyes.

Little red dots had appeared in the middle of the celery.

"What are these red dots?" she said.

## POP QUIZ
Why did Rachel think there was something wrong with her eyes?

ⓐ She could see red dots.
ⓑ She could not see anything.

"The stem is full of tiny tubes,"
said Grandmother.

"They suck up water in the same
way that you suck water through
a drinking straw."
Aha!

▲ a slice of celery

Rachel thought about cool drinks on a hot day.

She liked to drink them through a straw.

"The red dots show where the water has gone into the
tubes," said Grandmother.

"The tubes go all the way up through the stem and into
the leaf."

"So the tubes bring water to the leaf," said Rachel.

"But how does air get into the leaf?"

**KEY WORDS**

- drum
- grumble
- walk up and down the room
- complain
- lean back in one's chair

- at last
- no longer
- in the middle of
- tube
- drinking straw

Grandmother pushed her chair away from the table and stood up.

"Where are you going?" cried Rachel.

"We cannot stop now!"

"Be patient," said Grandmother as she walked into the next room.

There was a crash, and Rachel heard Grandmother muttering to herself.

What was she doing?

After a while, she came back with a large wooden box in her hand.

Grandmother lifted a microscope out of the box and set it on the table.

"With this, we can look very closely at the leaves," she said.

**KEY WORDS**

- **mutter to oneself**
- **wooden**
- **microscope**
- **set up** (set-set-set)

- **slide** (slide-slid-slid)
- **lens**
- **ready**
- **take a look**

- **run**
- **vein**
- **carry**

**46** • Chapter Three

She set up the microscope on the table and slid a leaf
beneath the glass lens.

"It is ready," she said. "You may take a look."

Rachel pressed her eye to the end of the microscope and
looked down it.

She saw something that looked like a wide green field
with rivers running through it.

"Those are called *veins*," said Grandmother. 

"They are just like the veins under your skin that take
blood through your body, but these veins carry water."

Rachel looked closer and saw tiny holes all over the leaf.

"What are these holes?" she asked.

"They let air in and out," said Grandmother.

"They can open wide or close tight."

Rachel looked up and asked, "Do they have a special name?"

Grandmother nodded.

"They are called *stomata*." Aha!

Rachel repeated the new word.

She felt clever because she knew the correct name for the tiny holes.

▲ stomata

**KEY WORDS**

- closer
- all over
- stomata
- repeat
- photosynthesis

"There is another word for you to learn," said
Grandmother.

"It is a long and difficult word. Not everyone can say it."

"What is it?" asked Rachel.

"It is *photosynthesis*.

It means *making something with light*," said
Grandmother.

"Photo..." Rachel tried to say the difficult word.

"Photo...syn...the...sis. Photo...synthesis. I can say it!"

Grandmother patted Rachel's shoulder.

"Now I think you are ready to win that contest.

Would you like a steamed dumpling to celebrate?"

There was a sudden shout from the window.

Harry jumped up from below the sill.

"Now I know that my machine needs water, sunlight, and holes to let air in," he shouted.

"Thank you for telling me how to win the contest!" Aha!

Before Rachel could stop him, he ran away down the garden path.

**POP QUIZ**

Write three things which the machine needs.

→ w________, s________, h________ for air

**KEY WORDS**

- pat
- celebrate
- below
- sill

# Comprehension Quiz

Chapter Three

**A** Put the sentences in order.

❶ Grandmother put the end of the celery into the water.

❷ Red dots appeared in the stem.

❸ Grandmother snapped the celery stem in two.

❹ Grandmother put red food dye in the water.

_____ → _____ → _____ → _____

**B** Choose the best answer to each question.

❶ Where in the plant is the food made?

a) the roots                             b) the fruit

c) the leaves                            d) the flowers

❷ Why were there red dots on the celery?

a) There was something wrong with Rachel's eyes.

b) The celery had a disease.

c) Rachel had drawn them on with her colored pencils.

d) The tiny tubes in the celery had begun to suck up the red water.

C Solve the crossword puzzle.

**Across** ❷ Chlorophyll traps this.

❸ The plant sucks it up through the stem in tiny tubes.

❹ These are tiny holes in the leaf to let air in and out.

❺ They take water from the soil.

❻ They take blood in the human body or water to the leaves of plants.

**Down** ❶ This is used to look at very small things.

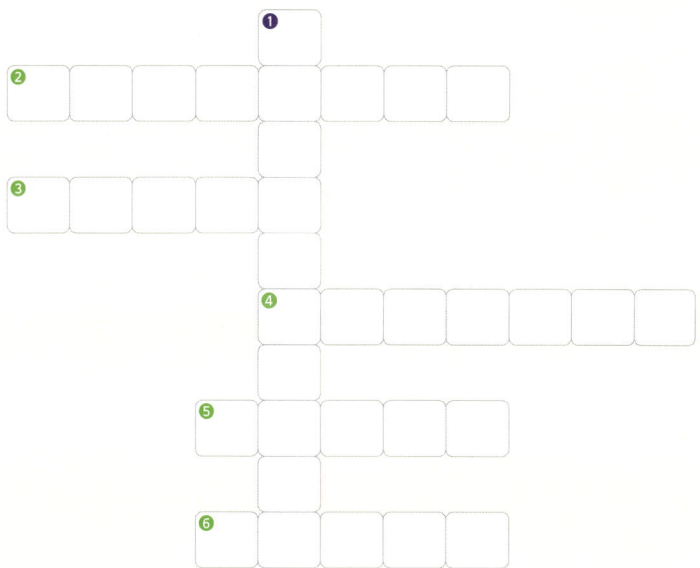

# Chapter Four

# The Incredible, Edible, Green Machine

It was the day of the contest.

All the children were excited.

Their parents waited at the edge of the room.

Each child stood behind a table with his or her machine on it for everyone to see.

Only Rachel's entry was hidden beneath a cloth.

Nobody would see it until she was ready.

Mrs. Young came in, followed by a scientist from the university.

"This is Professor Wilson," she said.

"He will decide who the winner is."

Professor Wilson had white hair and a kind face.

He peered over his glasses at Rachel and winked at her.

"Do you have a secret beneath that cloth?" he said.

"How exciting!"

KEY WORDS

- incredible
- entry
- be hidden
- followed by
- peer over
- wink at

Rachel's heart began to beat faster.

Her table was at the very end of the room, so the

professor would come to her last.

She looked over at her parents.

Grandmother sat with them.

She smiled and waved at Rachel.

She was wearing a new hat.

It was decorated with leaves. 📖 Aha!

Harry stood at the table next to Rachel.

He had made a big metal machine.

It looked like a box with lots of

small holes in it.

**KEY WORDS**

- **beat** (beat-beat-beaten)
- **faster**
- **very**
- **wave at**
- **next to**
- **metal**
- **go round**
- **stomach**
- **thousand**
- **wriggle**

**56** • Chapter Four

Professor Wilson went round the room and looked at all the machines.

He nodded a lot and wrote things down in a notebook.

As he got closer, Rachel's stomach began to feel strange.

It felt as though a thousand caterpillars were wriggling around inside.

Rachel looked at Harry.

He was tapping his machine and making sure it would work.

"Good luck," she said to him.

She waited for him to say the same thing back to her.

But Harry said, "I do not need good luck.

My machine is the best!"

Rachel was so angry that she wanted to tip over his table and break his machine.

Instead, she clenched her fists and took a deep breath.

At last, Professor Wilson reached Harry's table.

"Will you show me how your machine works?" he said.

Harry switched on a lamp.

It shone a bright light onto the machine.

"Air comes in here," he said as he pointed at the holes.

"If I pour in some water, my machine will make sugar."

He pointed to a slot in the side of the machine and put
an empty dish beneath it.

Harry took a jug of water and poured it into a tube at
one end of the machine.

Everyone watched to see what would happen.

Nothing came out of the slot.

The dish was still empty.

**POP QUIZ**

**Where did Harry pour a jug of water?**

ⓐ into the slot of the machine
ⓑ into the tube of the machine

**KEY WORDS**

- make sure
- Good luck.
- tip over
- instead

- clench one's fists
- take a deep breath
- switch on
- slot

- empty
- a jug of water

Professor Wilson waited.

Mrs. Young waited.

Rachel and everyone in the room waited.

Suddenly, there was a loud BANG.

Black smoke poured from the machine, and there was a horrid burning smell.

Grandmother screamed, and one of the younger children burst into tears.

Professor Wilson wrote something in his notebook.

Then, he walked over to Rachel's table.

"So this is the final machine," he said.

"I hope it is better than the last one."

POP QUIZ

What came out of Harry's machine?

ⓐ smoke

ⓑ sugar

**KEY WORDS**

- bang
- horrid
- burning
- younger

- burst into tears (burst-burst-burst)
- walk over to
- last

"Here is the Incredible, Edible, Green Machine," said
Rachel in a loud voice.

She took a deep breath and lifted the cloth.

Beneath the cloth was a tomato plant.

It was just a small one in an ordinary pot.

Some people began to laugh, and even Harry joined in.

"Quiet, please!" said Mrs. Young with a frown.

The professor turned to Rachel and said, "Why have you brought a plant to the contest?"

"This plant is the most incredible thing on our planet," said Rachel.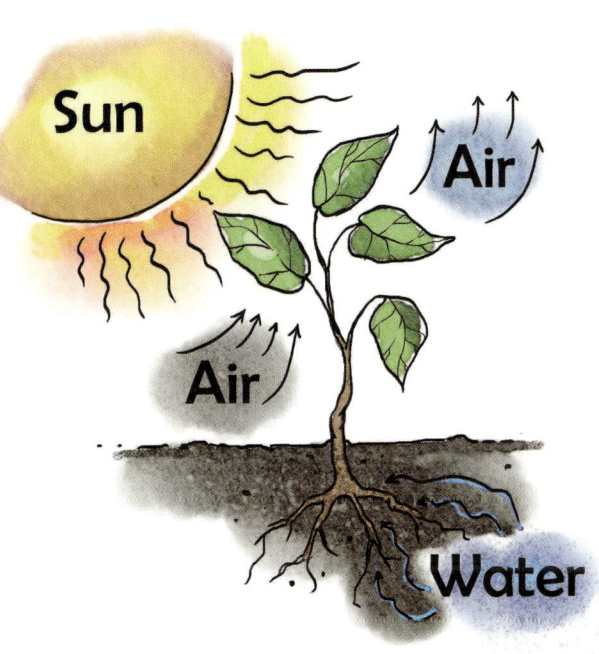

"It uses sunlight to make food from water and air."

She held up a diagram so that everyone could see it.

"The roots suck up water from the soil.

Then, tiny tubes take the water to the leaves. Air comes into the leaves through tiny holes like eyes that open and close."

**KEY WORDS**
- ordinary
- pot
- with a frown
- planet

Harry was not laughing now.

His face was almost as red as the tomatoes on the plant.

"The leaves make a sugary food," said Rachel.

"The food goes to the roots, the stem, and the fruit."

She picked a ripe, juicy tomato and put it in her mouth.

"It is incredible, it is edible, and it tastes delicious!"

The professor tapped his pen against his notebook.

"Tell me one thing," he said.

"Do you know the correct word for this?

The word that means *making something from light*?"

Rachel quickly swallowed the tomato.

She tried to remember that difficult word.

"Ph..." she began. "Photo..."

What was the second part of the word?

Her hands began to sweat.

"Say it a little at a time," she told herself.

"Photo...syn...the...sis," she said in a rush.

"Photosynthesis!"

**KEY WORDS**

- sugary
- ripe
- against

- quickly
- swallow
- sweat

- a little at a time
- in a rush

"I think we have a winner!" shouted the professor.

Everyone began to clap and cheer.

Only Harry did not join in.

Rachel felt a tiny bit sorry for him—but not much.

"Never mind," she said.

"You can have a prize as well."

Harry looked up.

"I can?" he said in surprise. Aha!

"Yes. Have a tomato!"

She took a ripe, squishy red tomato and pressed it against his nose.

Everyone burst out laughing.

Harry would never cheat again.

**A** Match each line with the right person.

 ❶ •

• a) "I think we have a winner!"

 ❷ •

• b) "My machine is the best."

 ❸ •

• c) "Quiet, please!"

**B** Put the sentences in order.

❶ Harry poured water into his machine.

❷ Harry switched on a lamp.

❸ Harry put an empty dish beneath the slot.

❹ There was a loud bang.

_____ → _____ → _____ → _____

**C** Choose the best answer to each question.

❶ Why did Rachel's stomach feel strange?

a) She was nervous.

b) She had eaten some caterpillars.

c) She had eaten too much breakfast.

d) Harry's machine was making her ill.

❷ Why did Rachel feel a tiny bit sorry for Harry—but not much?

a) She was an unkind person.

b) She thought his machine was the best.

c) She thought he might feel sad, but he didn't deserve to win.

d) She was too proud of winning to think about his feelings.

**D** Mark T for true or F for false.

❶ The plants had appeared by magic. T F

❷ The plants can make food out of air and water. T F

❸ Air comes into the leaves through tiny tubes. T F

❹ The food which the plants make goes to the roots, the stem, and the fruit. T F

# Let's Review the Story

Fill in the blanks to review the story.

**Title:** The [        ], Green [        ]

**Main Idea:**
Plants make food from a [        ]
and w [        ].

**Detail:**
- Air enters the plant by small
  [        ] in the leaves, called
  s [        ].
- Water enters the plant by
  [        ], which suck it up
  from the soil.
- The plant needs l [        ] to
  make food.

**Summary:**
The name of this process is
p [        ].

**Settings**

❶ S [        ]
- The teacher announces a
  contest.

❷ [        ]'s Home
- Rachel stays awake all night
  and draws.
- Harry looks through the
  window.

❸ The F [        ]
- Rachel realizes that plants
  make food from air and
  water.
- She hears a sound in the trees
  and runs away.

❹ [        ]'s House
- Rachel learns all about
  plants.
- Harry listens to their
  conversation.

# Let's Think & Talk

Think about the following questions and answer them freely.

❶ What are plants made of? Organize them and say.

❷ Find out what plants need to make their own nourishment and describe the process to make it. Draw pictures and make a presentation.

❸ Think about the vegetables that we eat and tell us which part of a plant that vegetable is. Do we eat the fruit, the leaf, the stem, or the root?

❹ Have you ever grown a plant by yourself? Tell us about the process of growing a plant.

# Let's Review the Story

**Title:** The [ Edible ], Green [ Machine ]

**Main Idea:**

Plants make food from [ air ] and [ water ].

**Detail:**

- Air enters the plant by small [ holes ] in the leaves, called [ stomata ].
- Water enters the plant by [ roots ], which suck it up from the soil.
- The plant needs [ light ] to make food.

**Summary:**

The name of this process is [ photosynthesis ].

**Settings**

❶ [ School ]
  - The teacher announces a contest.

❷ [ Rachel ]'s Home
  - Rachel stays awake all night and draws.
  - Harry looks through the window.

❸ The [ Forest ]
  - Rachel realizes that plants make food from air and water.
  - She hears a sound in the trees and runs away.

❹ [ Grandmother ]'s House
  - Rachel learns all about plants.
  - Harry listens to their conversation.

Smart Readers: **Wise & Wide**

# After-reading **Test**

- The Edible, Green Machine
- Level 4
- 27 Questions

(Vocabulary 7 / Reading Comprehension 16 /

Sentence Structure & Grammar 4)

1. Which of the following is the wrong past tense form of the verb?
   ① sat
   ② tore
   ③ shone
   ④ hide

2. Which of the following words is NOT done with eyes?
   ① peer
   ② wink
   ③ look
   ④ clench

3. Which of the following is similar to the word "dull"?
   ① sad
   ② boring
   ③ interesting
   ④ exciting

4. Which of these words means "alert"?

   In order to stay alert, she decided to go for a walk.

   ① awake
   ② slim
   ③ healthy
   ④ fit

5. What does the word "edible" mean?
  ① It grows in the ground.
  ② You can eat it.
  ③ It is amazing.
  ④ It comes from a plant.

6. What is the common word for the two blanks?

  • Rachel broke _____ a spinach leaf.
  • She pulled it _____ the plant.

  ① on                    ② to
  ③ for                   ④ off

7. What are the proper words for the blanks?

  • You were spying _____ me.
  • She set _____ the microscope on the table.

  ① in – for
  ② on – with
  ③ on – up
  ④ with – in

8. How did Rachel feel when Mrs. Young said about the prize for the winner?
  ① excited
  ② ill
  ③ angry
  ④ sleepy

9. Why did Rachel NOT go to school on the second day?

   ① She was ill.

   ② She was tired.

   ③ It was the weekend.

   ④ It was her birthday.


10. Which character is speaking this?

> "I really want to win this prize because I love the botanic gardens."

   ① Mrs. Young

   ② Harry

   ③ Rachel's mother

   ④ Rachel


11. What is NOT true about Grandmother?

   ① She was old.

   ② She knew a lot about plants.

   ③ She liked to cook.

   ④ She could not sing.


12. Who was watching Grandmother and Rachel from over the fence?

   ① a deer

   ② Mrs. Young

   ③ Rachel's mother

   ④ Harry


13. What is NOT a fruit?

   ① tomato

   ② spinach

   ③ zucchini

   ④ cucumber

14. What did Rachel look at under the microscope?

    ① some skin

    ② a leaf

    ③ a root of an onion

    ④ a stem of a celery


15. What does chlorophyll do?

    ① It captures sunlight in the leaves.

    ② It makes the plant taste good.

    ③ It sucks up water from the ground.

    ④ It produces flowers.


16. Where does a plant get water from?

    ① from the air

    ② from animals licking it

    ③ from juicy fruits

    ④ from the soil


17. Why did Grandmother put red food dye in the water?

    ① to make it look pretty

    ② to show Rachel where the water went

    ③ to make it taste good

    ④ to make celery soup


18. Why do you think the holes in the leaves are like eyes?

    ① They are big enough to see.

    ② They have eyelashes.

    ③ They open and close.

    ④ They are different colors.

19. Why did Rachel say that she might NOT enter the contest?
 ① She was tired of learning about plants.
 ② She wanted Harry to go away.
 ③ She was not good at inventing something.
 ④ Harry begged her not to enter the contest.


20. Which statement is NOT true about Professor Wilson?
 ① He had white hair.
 ② He wore glasses.
 ③ He had an angry face.
 ④ He was a scientist.


※ Choose each sentence that does NOT match the story. (21~23)
21. ① Rachel pinched her cheek to wake up.
 ② Rachel thought about the contest all the way home.
 ③ Rachel sat at the back of her class and yawned.
 ④ Rachel looked down at the berries in her hand.


22. ① Rachel's entry was hidden beneath a cloth.
 ② Harry put an empty dish beneath the slot in his machine.
 ③ Harry poured water into the tiny bottle.
 ④ Rachel pressed the tomato against Harry's nose.


23. ① Grandmother dug in the soil.
 ② Rachel cut a zucchini in half.
 ③ Harry knew where Rachel lived.
 ④ Mrs. Young decided who the winner was.

※ Choose the wrong part of each sentence. (24~25)

24.
He wanted always to win every contest there was.
         ①        ②       ③      ④

25.
There must be wrong something with her eyes.
      ① ②      ③       ④

※ Choose the correct word for each blank. (26~27)

26.
Her skin was _____ wrinkled as a raisin.

① so                   ② as
③ like                ④ of

27.
Rachel knew that plants grew _____ better on warm, sunny days.

① much              ② so
③ such              ④ too

**Sarah J. Dodd**

Sarah J. Dodd is an experienced primary school teacher who resides in the UK, but has also taught in Australia. She has a PhD in Science and a certificate in Creative Writing. She has published four books for younger children — 'An Angel Anyway' (Anyway Press) and the Little Angels' series (Lion Hudson plc). Her children's Bible will be published in 2015. She is currently working on a novel for 9-12 year olds and another for young adults.

 **Smart Readers Wise & Wide 4-2**

# The Edible, Green Machine

Written by Sarah J. Dodd
Illustrated by Nika Tchaikovskaya

First Published in December 2014

Editorial Manager: Juyon Choi
Editors: Kyunghee Jang, Jiyeong Park
Designer: Eunhee Lee
Cover Designer: Eunhee Lee

Published and distributed by

 Happy House

Darakwon Bldg., 64-1 Jandari-ro, Mapo-gu, Seoul, Korea 121-894
Tel: 82-2-736-2031(ext. 250)     Fax: 82-2-736-2037
Homepage: www.ihappyhouse.co.kr
Publisher: Kyudo Chung

Copyright © Darakwon Publishing Company 2014
English Edition published 2014, by arrangement with Darakwon, by Happy House
English Edition Copyright © 2014, Happy House

ISBN: 978-89-6653-165-3 18740 / 978-89-6653-156-1 18740(set)

[Components]
• 1 Audio CD (Recording Studio: Aram)
• Answer Keys & Korean Translation: Free download at www.ihappyhouse.co.kr